Parent's Introduction

Whether your child is a beginning reader, a reluctant reader, or an eager reader, this book offers a fun and easy way to encourage and help your child in reading.

Developed with reading education specialists, *We Both Read* books invite you and your child to take turns reading aloud. You read the left-hand pages of the book, and your child reads the right-hand pages—which have been written at one of six early reading levels. The result is a wonderful new reading experience and faster reading development!

You may find it helpful to read the entire book aloud yourself the first time, then invite your child to participate the second time. As you read, try to make the story come alive by reading with expression. This will help to model good fluency. It will also be helpful to stop at various points to discuss what you are reading. This will help increase your child's understanding of what is being read.

In some books, a few challenging words are introduced in the parent's text, distinguished with **bold** lettering. Pointing out and discussing these words can help to build your child's reading vocabulary. If your child is a beginning reader, it may be helpful to run a finger under the text as each of you reads. Please also notice that a "talking parent" ⊙ icon precedes the parent's text, and a "talking child" ⊙ icon precedes the child's text.

If your child struggles with a word, you can encourage "sounding it out," but keep in mind that not all words can be sounded out. Your child might pick up clues about a word from the picture, other words in the sentence, or any rhyming patterns. If your child struggles with a word for more than five seconds, it is usually best to simply say the word.

Most of all, remember to praise your child's efforts and keep the reading fun. After you have finished the book, ask a few questions and discuss what you have read together. Rereading this book multiple times may also be helpful for your child.

Try to keep the tips above in mind as you read together, but don't worry about doing everything right. Simply sharing the enjoyment of reading together will increase your child's reading skills and help to start your child off on a lifetime of reading enjoyment!

We Both Read: Happy and Healthy

---

*With special thanks to Dr. Ronald Bachman, M.D. for his advice
and recommendations on this book*

Use of photographs provided by Getty Images © Copyright 2002

We Both Read® is a registered trademark of Treasure Bay, Inc.

Published by Treasure Bay, Inc.
P.O. Box 119
Novato, CA 94948 USA

Printed in Singapore

Library of Congress Catalog Card Number: 2002094714

Hardcover ISBN: 978-1-891327-47-6
Paperback ISBN: 978-1-891327-48-3

We Both Read® Books
Patent No. 5,957,693

Visit us online at:
www.WeBothRead.com

PR 2-11

Happy and Healthy

By Sindy McKay

TREASURE BAY

Run like the wind! Throw to the moon! Jump to the sky! Almost anything is possible when you're **healthy** and strong.

 It feels good to be **healthy.**

And it's not hard.

In fact, it can be lots of fun!

 When you are healthy, you are full of **energy**. You feel like you can do anything!

 **Energy** keeps you going through the day.

You need energy to work.

You need energy to play.

   Energy comes from the food that you eat. A balanced diet that includes a variety of fresh, delicious, healthy food supplies the body with the kind of **fuel** it needs to keep it going fast and strong.

 Good food is good **fuel.**

It keeps your body going all day long.

 For most of us the most important meal of the day is breakfast. When we wake up in the morning, it has been over ten hours since the last time we ate. Our fuel is running low and our brains and bodies need an energy **boost.**

A healthy snack can give us a **boost** between meals. Fruit makes a great healthy snack.

Good, healthy food provides you with the protein, carbo-hydrates, fats, vitamins, and minerals that your body needs. But don't forget that **water** is important too.

You can get some of the water you need from delicious drinks like milk and juice. But be sure to also include several glasses of water in your diet everyday.

 **Water** is very good for you.

You should drink it every day.

You can play in it, too!

   **Exercise** is a huge part of staying healthy. It keeps our
bodies fit and our minds alert.

When you **exercise** every day,
you feel really good.

   Exercise benefits your body in many ways. It helps your heart work more efficiently. It builds your **muscles** to make you strong. It keeps you stretched and flexible.

 Strong **muscles** are important.

When you are strong,

you can play all day!

 There are many ways to get the **exercise** you need every day. Playing sports, skipping rope, raking leaves, and vacuuming the living room carpet are just a few of the ways to get your body moving and your blood pumping.

◔ **Exercise** should be fun.

Try to find the kind of exercise

that is fun for you.

 Spending the day outdoors with your **family** is a fantastic way to stay fit.

Bike riding is an activity that just about everyone can do, no matter what age. So get out in the sunshine and ride!

 Football is a great game to play with the **family.**
You run. You throw. You have a great time!

 You can keep active all year long, even in the winter when it's cold outside and there's snow on the ground. Build a snowman or go ice-skating or help your parents shovel the snow.

Try to get your whole family out to exercise. It will help keep everyone healthy.

 Playing with your **friends** is one of the best ways to get exercise without even trying. Your local park probably has a playground with all kinds of equipment that helps you build your muscles while having a great time.

Some parks have a pool you can use. Take your **friends** to the pool and make a big splash!

You don't need fancy **equipment** to have a great time with your friends. Grab a rope and start jumping. Mark off a hopscotch court and start hopping. Pull on your skates and hit the ice.

Tag is a great game to play with your friends.
You don't need any **equipment** to play this game.
You just need to run fast.

 Team sports are a great way to help you stay healthy and fit. A good coach will make sure that everyone on the team gets a chance to play and has a good time.

It's fun to play on a team.

You make lots of good friends.

You might even win sometimes!

 It is just as important to **relax** sometimes as is it to exercise. Your body and brain need some time to rest up for the next adventure of the day. Sometimes it's good to just do nothing at all.

There are many ways to **relax.**

You can read a book.

You can play cards.

You can lie in the grass and look at the sky.

Everything that is living needs to sleep. When you are **tired,** it's hard to think and it's hard to play. Getting **enough** rest every night gives your brain and body time to recharge so you'll be ready to play hard again tomorrow.

Sometimes you don't get **enough** sleep at night.
The next day you are very **tired**.

Another important step on the road to good health is to visit your health care professionals on a regular basis.

Your family doctor will make sure your body is in good working condition. Your family **dentist** will check your mouth, gums, and teeth to detect any potential problems.

Your **dentist** will sometimes clean your teeth. You can help keep them clean by brushing after every meal.

When you visit your doctor, he or she will probably ask you many **questions** about how you are feeling and what's going on in your life. Then your doctor will work with you to correct any problems you might have.

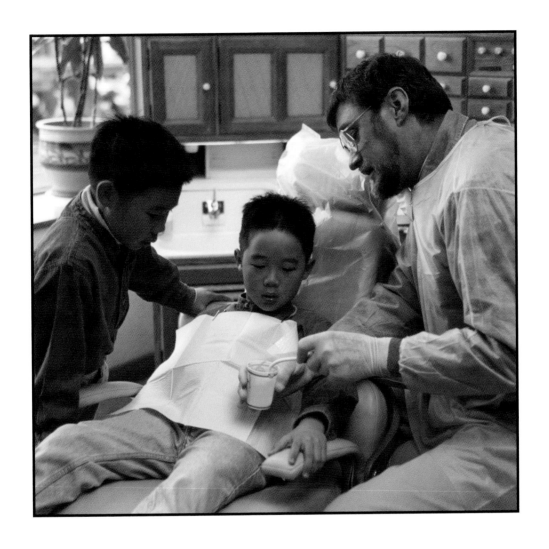

 You might have **questions** for your
doctor or dentist.

Don't be afraid to ask.

He or she will try to answer them.

   No matter how well you take care of yourself, you will probably get sick sometimes.

If you do get sick, try to keep your germs to yourself! Cover your mouth when you cough or sneeze. Don't share your drinking glass with your friends. Stay home until you are feeling better.

Everyone gets sick sometimes.
But you will feel better faster,
if you take care of yourself.

   It takes just a few simple steps to be as healthy as you can be. Exercise, eat right, drink plenty of water, get enough rest, and see your doctor and dentist regularly.

Friends and family are important, too.

They help us stay healthy and happy.

   When you are fit and strong, you feel good about yourself. You are happy knowing you are the best person you can be, no matter what your shape or size or natural abilities. You're ready to face each new day with energy and enthusiasm.

 Be healthy.

Be happy.

And have fun!

If you liked
Happy and Heathy, **here are two other**
We Both Read® **Books you are sure to enjoy!**

When Jason gets sick, he is told that he has to stay home and get better. But he is supposed to pitch in an important game in a few days! In this light-hearted book Jason must deal with the same frustrations and disappointments that all children experience when they have to stay home with a cold or flu.

To see all the We Both Read books that are available,
just go online to **www.webothread.com**

Explore the mystery and wonder of the tropical rain
forest! Travel around the equator to Africa, Asia,
and South America discovering the world's most
fascinating plant and animal life. Captivating photographs, along with compelling text, make this Level
1–2 book an exciting adventure and a great learning
experience.